Know Your Donkeys

Jack Byard

Old Pond Publishing

First published 2010, reprinted 2011

ISBN 978-1-906853-31-0

Published by:
Old Pond Publishing Ltd
Dencora Business Centre
36 White House Road
Ipswich IP1 5LT
United Kingdom

www.oldpond.com

Book design by Liz Whatling
Printed and bound in China

Contents

Measurements are given in 'hh' meaning 'hands high'. For more information see 'Donkey Talk' at the end of the book.

Acknowledgements

I would like to thank the following organisations without whose help
Know Your Donkeys would never have been written.

The Donkey Sanctuary and *NEDDI* in England, *The Donkey Sanctuary* in Cyprus,
El Refugio del Burrito in Spain and *Il Rifugio degli Asinelli* in Italy.

Many thanks also go to Beate Scherf at the Food and Agriculture Organisation of the United Nations
(FAO) for her help sourcing information and photographs; to Tony Harman of Maple Leaf Images in
Skipton for his advice on the finer points of photographs and to the many people throughout Britain,
Europe, the USA and Canada for all their assistance with pictures and information.
Thanks finally to Rebecca who keeps Grandad's feet firmly on the ground.
Any mistakes are mine and mine alone.

Picture Credits

(1) Don and Michelle Owens, Four Spokes Ranch, *(2)* The American Donkey and Mule Society, *(3)* Frank and Betsy Burke of
www.lazybspotteddonkeys.com in Texas, *(4)* Nancy Kerson, mustangs4us.com, *(5)* Mr G Catillo, *(6)* El Refugio del Burrito, *(7)* Daniele Bigi,
(8) Associació de Criadors de Pura Raça Asenca de les Illes Balears, *(9)* Ursula Bivans, *(10)* Uli Harder, *(11)* Grosbois F. Haras Nationaux,
(12) Izzet Zorlu, *(13)* Association para la Defense del Burro, *(14)* Rivalain Y. Haras Natiobaux, *(15)* Helen McCann, *(16)* Jan Morse,
(17) SOO…Grupo para la Conservación Formento del Burro Majorero, *(18)* Terra Degli Asini – Lissaro, Italy, *(19)* Food and Agricultural
Organisation of the United Nations, *(20)* Penny Cooke, *(21)* Grosbois F. Haras Nationaux, *(22)* Netanel Nickalls, *(23)* Archivio RARE,
(24) Annie Pollock, *(25)* The Donkey Sanctuary, *(26)* Ursula Bivans, *(27)* Archivio RARE, *(28)* Fattorie Faggioli, *(29)* Daniele Bigi,
(30) Marwell Wildlife, *(31)* El Refugio del Burrito, *(32)* Colchester Zoo, *(33)* Knute's Kustom Mule Kompany, Rod and Becky Knutson
(34) Knute's Kustom Mule Kompany, Rod and Becky Knutson.

Foreword

Although donkeys – also known as asses – are members of the horse family, they are genetically different from horses themselves. During my research for this book I came to realise that the donkey genus includes many distinctive breeds.

I have also come to appreciate the historical roles played by these sturdy, adaptable creatures in almost every corner of the world. Whether they pulled a farmer's plough, carried the equipment for wars, were ridden or driven as transport or were simply kept for their milk, it is difficult to imagine where we might have been without them.

Sadly, the mechanisation of farming in the 20th century led to a reduced need for working donkeys. Today a number of traditional breeds

are verging on extinction although breeders and governments are setting up programmes to reverse this trend. Ever versatile, the donkey has now found new vocations in the tourist industry and as valuable support in animal-assisted therapies.

Donkeys and mules are highly intelligent animals that have a great sense of self preservation – which may seem like stubbornness. If they are unsure of what they are being asked to do, they just don't do it.

JACK BYARD
2010

1.

Abyssinian

Native to
Ethiopia

Size
12hh on average

The Abyssinian is tan to grey with a pale grey underbelly, inner thighs and muzzle. The ear-surround is dark as are the tips of the mane. They have a dorsal stripe and cross.

The Abyssinian lives mainly in desert areas that vary from below sea level to 700 metres above and where rainfall seldom exceeds 200 mm a year. They have developed the ability to survive on poor-quality grass and forage. They live in small groups of up to five animals with the number depending on the quantity of food and water available.

In some areas Abyssinian donkeys are used for food which, added to the competition with domestic livestock for food and water, has caused a 90% reduction in numbers. Their milk is said to be good for skin conditions or for those who are lactose intolerant.

The breed is critically endangered. They are now used in protected areas for transporting all manner of goods, from food and water to fuel and building materials.

American Mammoth

Native to
America

Size
There is no standard size

Description

The American Mammoth can be black, chestnut, spotted, dun, white, dapple-grey or palomino.

In America, before the days of mechanisation, most of the power for transport and agriculture came from the donkey so the larger and stronger they were, the better. The native donkeys were in need of improvement and the European breeds chosen for this mammoth task (excuse the pun), were the Catalan, Andalusian, Majorcan and Maltese. It was recorded that by 1890 the demand for Majorcan (now Balear) donkeys was such that their native area was almost cleared of stock. George Washington is credited with developing the American Mammoth.

The coming of mechanisation in transport and agriculture meant there was no longer a use for this sturdy, reliable giant. As a result many thousands were slaughtered. A few breeders were able to hold onto their stock so, although the breed is rare, it is safe from extinction.

American Spotted

Native to
Probably Mexico

Size
9hh-16hh

Description

The American Spotted can be any donkey colour as long as the main body colour is broken with white patches that cover somewhere between 5% and 99% of its body.

It is widely believed that the American Spotted donkey originated with the American Wild Burro. Prior to this the American donkey was dark brown, black or roan. The Wild Burro was a smaller animal but with a much larger range of colours including, you guessed it, spotted. These two breeds were crossed to create the impressive American Spotted.

This lovely animal has been grazing the fields of America since the 1700s. In the early days it was used entirely as a work animal as it was considered not suitable for any other purpose. The American Spotted is still used as a working animal today but is also used in harness, under saddle and to sire colourful mules.

Donkeys, including the American Spotted, have an aversion to intruders, a trait which can be put to good use for guarding sheep and cattle.

American Wild Burro

Native to
The deserts of North America

Size
11hh on average

Description

They are normally grey but sometimes black or brown. Most of them have pale underbellies. They usually have a dorsal stripe and cross, leg stripes and a dark outline to the ears.

The Wild Burro was introduced into the south-west deserts of America by the Spanish in the 16th century. Burro is the traditional Mexican name for 'donkey'. As a pack animal they were in great demand in this arid countryside because of their ability to survive on low-quality forage and little water. The Burro can sustain a water loss of up to 30% of their body weight and replenish it with a 5-minute drink.

The gold and silver prospectors of old who crossed the desert relied on this sturdy breed to carry their supplies. In many cases the Burro would survive while the prospector would be beaten by the harsh desert conditions.

In 1971 Congress unanimously passed the Wild Free-Roaming Act which gave federal protection to the wild burro and mustang populations, making it illegal to harass, brand, capture or kill these animals.

5.

Amiata

Native to
Italy

Size
12.2hh – 13hh

Description

They are mouse-grey with a pale grey underbelly and muzzle. They sometimes have white on the inner legs, throat and around the eyes. The ears have black edges and there is a well-defined dorsal stripe and cross. Dark stripes can occasionally be found on the legs.

The Amiata donkey was introduced to the Amiata mountains in Italy by maritime traders about 2,000 BC. Until the latter part of the 19th century they were a common site in the Tuscan mountains. This wiry donkey was and still is, although in a much reduced way, used on farms as a pack animal or for transport. It is an ideal working companion in these mountainous regions.

At the beginning of the 20th century there were about 2,500 Amiata donkeys. Numbers declined for various reasons and reached an all-time low between 1970 and 1980. In 2003 only around 200 breeding Amiata survived. There is now an extensive breeding programme in place and the situation is improving. The Amiata is currently used for work in inaccessible forest areas or to carry packs for walkers. Their milk is used in various beauty products.

Andalusian

Native to
Spain

Size
13.2hh – 15.1hh

Description

They are either grey-spotted, a shade of grey or strawberry roan. They rarely have the dorsal stripe and cross.

The Andalusian is thought by many to be the oldest European breed of donkey, having arrived in Spain over 3,000 years ago. They are descendants of a now-extinct breed of large Egyptian donkey known as the Pharaoh.

The breed was mainly used on farms in the El Guadalquivir region of Spain. The farmers required a strong and docile animal which could work in the cork forests and citrus groves and produce good mules.

The Andalusian has a good resistance to disease and adapts well to arid conditions. It has boundless energy and is long lived. Despite these excellent qualities, in the 1980s the breed was almost extinct with mechanisation being the main cause of the decline. The breed numbers were estimated at 120-150 worldwide. A number of organisations are now working to save this handsome, gentle animal from extinction.

Asinara

Native to
The Island of Asinara off the north-west coast of Sardinia.

Size
7.3hh – 10.1hh

Description

The Asinara appears albino. It is white all over with pink skin visible through the hair. The muzzle has no hair and the hooves are without pigment. The irises are pink or blue. It is, however, only considered a 'partial incomplete albino' since there are just a few grey animals.

It is believed that the Asinara is descended from a group of white donkeys imported from Egypt in the 1800s by the Marquis de Mores (the Duke of Asinara). The breed is hardy and has the ability to live off meagre grazing, which is very fortunate since fresh water and quality vegetation are in short supply on Asinara. This small, rugged animal manages to survive and multiply in this harsh environment.

The human inhabitants were forced to leave Asinara in the late 1800s and went to live in Stintino, on the coast of Sardinia, leaving the donkeys to fend for themselves. Asinara is now part of the Italian National Parks system and the animals are under the care and protection of the Sardinian Forestry Agency and the Faculty of Veterinary Medicine in Sassari.

Balear

Native to
Spain

Size
14.2hh – 15hh

Description

They are black or almost black with a pale grey around the mouth, eyes, muzzle and underbelly.

It is believed by many that this European donkey has its origins in the western Mediterranean from where it spread into southern Europe. In 2005 the breed known as the Mallorquin or the Majorcan officially became known as the Balear. It is noted for being strong and healthy with a slightly nervous temperament. The females were used mainly as draught animals, carrying crops of olives, producing the power for the corn mills and for transporting the farmer and his family. The male was dedicated to mule breeding and used to produce the Kentucky mule which is noted for its size and strength.

As with most donkeys, numbers declined with the increase in mechanisation and extinction was a distinct possibility. In 1990 the government and a group of farmers led the fight back with a core of fifty animals. In 2002 they founded an organisation (ACRIPROASMA) and created a stud book. The breed is now used in the conservation and maintenance of wood and scrub land.

9.

Bourbonnais

Native to
France

Size
13.1hh – 14.1hh

Description

The body is beige to chocolate-brown while the muzzle and underbelly are grey, as are the spectacle markings around the eyes. The dorsal stripe and cross are a darker brown. The legs can have horizontal stripes.

The Bourbonnais comes from Allier in Auvergne, France, where it was depicted on a frieze in the church of St. Julien which dates from the early 12th century. They helped in the maintenance of farms and vineyards and were also a big part of rural life in Allier, hauling supplies or produce and providing transport. In addition to its diet of grass, flowers and hay, the Bourbonnais drinks in the region of 15 litres of water a day.

This gentle donkey is healthy and long-lived: 30 to 40 years is normal but reaching 50 is not exceptional. Though on the endangered list, the Bourbonnais is becoming a success in the tourist industry. This sure-footed animal is ideal for trekking over rough terrain but is just as much at home with more gentle pursuits in harness or under saddle.

10.

Catalan

Native to
Catalonia in north-east Spain

Size
13.3hh

Description

The Catalan is black, turning to chestnut in the winter. They have a greyish-white underbelly, muzzle and spectacles.

The Catalan is a very old breed which is related to the Balear and the Zamorano Leones. It was once the main source of power on the farm. In its heyday there were in excess of 50,000 at work but at the last count numbers were down to 500, of which 400 were in Catalonia. A conservation programme is now in place and I understand that numbers are slowly increasing.

The Catalan is not known for its easy-going temperament but it is hard working, long-lived and remarkably disease resistant. To put it delicately, male Catalans are known for their enthusiasm for the female of the species. These positive attributes created a demand for its use in improving other breeds and it was used in the creation of the American Mammoth. The Catalan's ability as a draught and pack animal has won it many competitions and prizes.

11.

Cotentin

Native to
France

Size
11.3hh – 13.2hh

Description

The Cotentin is ash-grey, blue-grey or dove-grey, occasionally with a reddish tint on the head. The underbelly, insides of the forelegs, thighs, muzzle and spectacle markings are a greyish-white. They have a dorsal stripe, cross and possibly leg stripes.

For centuries the Cotentin, (pronounced *Ko-ton-tan*) has grazed and worked on the small farms of Lower Normandy. Just over a century ago the Manche area of Normandy had in the region of 9,000 donkeys which were used mainly as pack animals for transporting milk, hay, manure and the apples for making cider.

Mechanisation in agriculture means the Cotentin has disappeared from the countryside today but all is not lost. The breed has found a niche in tourism, especially trekking holidays where this gentle and willing animal makes an ideal companion.

The Cotentin is also used for Animal Assisted Therapy. This began in the British Isles in the 1700s but was championed by Florence Nightingale during the Crimean War because the sick and disabled can derive great benefit from the companionship of animals.

12.

Cypriot

Native to
Cyprus

Size
13hh on average

They are black, brown or grey with a black mane. They have a lighter underbelly and a cream muzzle and spectacles. Some have the dorsal stripe and cross.

The Cypriot or 'Karpas' donkey has a long history in Cyprus, a skeleton having been found in a tomb in the city of Enkomi. The ancient and the modern frequently meet on the roads of northern Cyprus where the donkey has not been entirely abandoned as transport. To own a donkey was once a luxury and apart from being the family transport they were used to carry olives and cereals to the mills. They were also used by the British army on the island during World War II.

The population of the wild Cypriot donkey increased after the Turkish intervention in 1974 when the Greek Cypriots were forced to abandon their animals. The donkeys were eventually taken to the remote and beautiful area of Karpas in north-east Cyprus where it was thought they would stand the best chance of survival.

13.

Encartaciones

Native to
Spain

Size
11.3hh

The Encartaciones is black or chestnut with lighter areas around the mouth and eyes and a white underbelly. They have small hooves and ears and occasionally dark stripes on the legs. They have a dark dorsal stripe and a tuft at the end of the tail.

This docile donkey from the Basque region of Spain has been known in the area since the 15th century. It has been the muscle power for the Spanish explorer, the military and the small farmer who used it to shepherd stock between winter and summer grazing or as a draught animal. This small donkey, only 120 cm tall, is still used on small Basque farms although mechanisation led to a dramatic fall in numbers and it is thought there are only 100 Encartaciones left today.

In 1996 ADEBUEN, (Association para la Defense del Burro Encartaciones), was created to protect and prevent a further fall in numbers. These small, strong animals have for centuries been the power helping create wealth for many. We cannot abandon them now.

Grand Noir du Berry

Native to
France

Size
12.3hh – 14.1hh

Description

The Grand Noir du Berry is black or a shade of bay. The underbelly, inside forelegs and thighs are a pale grey as are the spectacles.

In the mid 19th century there were almost 9,000 Grand Noir du Berry and they could be seen working on small farms and vineyards where they were the draught animal of choice. It was about the same time that the Grand Noir replaced the human draught animal to haul barges along the Berry canal and onwards to the Briare canal and Paris.

Within 100 years, mechanisation had brought the Grand Noir to the brink of extinction. It was the dedication of a small group of farmers in Lignières-en-Berry in conjunction with a campaign to save rural traditions which came to the rescue. By the year 2000, 1,000 Grand Noir du Berry were registered. Today the breed is mainly used in the leisure industry to carry equipment for tourists on trekking holidays. It is an ideal task for this strong yet docile animal.

Irish

Native to
Ireland

Size
13hh on average

Description

Irish donkeys are mainly brown or black with a dorsal stripe and cross.

The Irish donkey is not recognised as a specific breed but this little donkey has played such an important role in Irish history and established itself so soundly in the country's affections that I thought it deserved a page of its own.

It is strongly believed that donkeys arrived in the British Isles with the Roman armies almost 2,000 years ago. During the Peninsula War in Iberia (1808-1814) there was great demand for Irish horses. Donkeys from England were traded for these horses and records suggest that this is when the donkey became more visible in Ireland.

One line of my research suggests that in its early days in Ireland the donkey was owned solely by the wealthy and used for milk. There is mention of a single donkey being taken as spoils at the fall of Maynooth Castle in 1534. In later years this powerful donkey was used for ploughing, carrying or as transport.

16.

Kiang

Native to
Tibet, China and India

Size
13.3hh

Description

They are a dark chestnut in winter and a sleek reddish-brown in summer. The underbelly is white, as are the legs except for a brown stripe down the front. The short brown mane stands up vertically. A dark stripe runs down the spine.

The Kiang is the largest member of the wild ass family. It has the appearance of a horse, but the long thin tail with a tuft at the end and hairs growing up at the side give it away. They graze the Tibetan plateau at heights from 2,500 to 5,300 metres above sea level living mainly off the wispy, fine-textured Stipa grass and other low-growing vegetation.

During August and September they gain about 45 kg in weight and a thick coat to help them survive the harsh winters where temperatures range from -9°C to -35°C. Throughout the mating season vicious battles take place between the reigning stallion and the wannabees. The Kiang has only two predators: man and wolf. When under attack the herd will form a circle, lower their heads and kick out violently.

17.

Majorero

Native to
The Canary Islands

Size
10.3hh on average

Description

The Majorero is grey with a pale grey muzzle, underbelly, inner ear and spectacles. The ears have dark edges. They have a dorsal stripe and cross.

The Majorero arrived in the Canary Islands from north-west Africa in the 15th century where it has adapted to the volcanic environment. Like most donkey breeds, it is a born survivor and can endure harsh conditions with little food or water.

The Majorero is known for its vitality, health and strength. This gentle animal has been used, and still is to a lesser extent, as a pack animal, for pulling carts, ploughing fields and under saddle. They are now mainly used in recreational pursuits and tourism. At the last count the population was under 200 animals and since it is in danger of extinction it is now protected by the Agricultural Administration. The Majorero can live at least 30 years, so owning one is not a short-term commitment.

18.

Martina Franca

Native to
The Puglia region of Italy

Size
13.1hh – 15.3hh

Description

The Martina Franca is dark bay. The underbelly, inner thighs and muzzle are grey.

According to local Puglia inhabitants, this large donkey is descended from the original local breed which was crossed with the Catalonian donkeys imported into Puglia during the Spanish occupation. Another theory suggests that these local donkeys were crossed instead with fifteen Spanish donkeys imported by the Duke of Martina.

Between the 18th and 19th centuries the Martina Franca, then known as the Puglese, thrived. It was reared all over Italy and exported widely. It was not until 1904 that the Puglese was renamed the Martina Franca.

This strong and intelligent breed was used as a pack animal and to produce mules. Because of their ability to cope with poor pasture and rough terrain they were used by the Alpine troops to carry equipment over the difficult mountain passes. After World War II increased mechanisation meant that numbers began to fall. I understand that there is now a breeding programme to ensure the future of this historic animal.

Mary
aka
Maryiskaya

Native to
Turkmenistan, central Asia
and surrounding areas

Size
11.2hh – 15.3hh

Description

The Mary is most frequently grey but occasionally black. The underbelly is grey or white as are the insides of the forelegs and thighs. The legs have horizontal dark stripes. Most Marys have a dorsal stripe and cross.

Information about the origins of the Mary (as it is known in western countries) donkey is unclear. Today the Mary is bred largely in the Mary province and Ashkhabad region of Turkmenistan. It is extremely adaptable and able to survive in a harsh mountainous region or the lush regions of the plains. Their native countryside is inaccessible and it is necessary to transport goods over steep slopes and mountain tracks. The Mary walks with a short pace which reduces the swaying of a load and allows for steady progress on steep paths.

An improving rural economy and increased mechanisation led to a serious drop in numbers. However, the Mary is still used for expeditions and mountain rescue parties and a breeding programme has been put in place on reserves in the area to ensure the survival of this ancient breed.

20.

Mediterranean Miniature

Native to
Sicily and Sardinia

Size
8.1hh – 8.2hh

The Mediterranean Miniature is mainly grey-dun or a shade of grey. Less common colours are spotted, chestnut, white, dark brown and black. They have a lighter coloured underbelly and muzzle. The ears have a darker edging and there is a dark tip to the tail. The majority have the dorsal stripe and cross.

The Mediterranean Miniature is a naturally small donkey rather than bred down from a standard breed. They were once used as a draught animal and for grinding grain in peasants' houses. Blindfolded and harnessed to the mill, they would walk for hours in endless circles. History has not always treated donkeys kindly.

Today this friendly and intelligent donkey is kept as a pet. It makes a good companion animal for children or people with disabilities and is a welcome visitor in many nursing homes. They enjoy human company and will nudge you to gain attention. Many Mediterraneans are used to carry packs on camping trips and are easily trained to pull a small cart. The Mediterranean can live for 40 years.

21.

Normandy

Native to
France

Size
9hh – 12.1hh

Description

The Normandy is brown and occasionally mouse-grey. The underbelly, inside forelegs, thighs and muzzle are a greyish-white. The spectacle markings around the eyes sometimes have a hint of red. They have a dorsal stripe and cross.

The Normandy, like most French donkeys, worked in agriculture as a pack animal, carrying corn or hay and taking metal milk churns out to the fields at milking time. In 1997 there were 4,500 registered with the Ministry of Agriculture. It was also used in market gardening to carry produce to local markets. This small yet strong animal is capable of carrying the equivalent of its own weight, usually around 180 kg.

Today the Normandy is frequently used under saddle or in harness in their new role at seaside resorts, village fetes and in the tourist industry – not forgetting their popularity as pets.

The Association of Normandy Donkeys ensures that the natural strength and calm temperament of the breed are not undermined by careless breeding.

Onager

Native to
Mongolia, northern Iran,
Tibet, India and Pakistan

Size
12hh on average

Description

The Onager is reddish-brown in the summer and yellowish-brown in the winter. They have a black stripe with a white border down the middle of their back. The underbelly is buff, they have a dark upright mane, the ears have dark tips and the tail ends in a dark tassel. The legs are short.

The Onager is a descendant of the Asiatic Wild Ass. It is small and slender compared to many donkeys but what it lacks in size it makes up for in speed and endurance, being capable of a constant 40 mph over a 15-mile stretch. The world's expert on the breed told me that despite tales to the contrary, the Onager has never been domesticated. In Hebrew it is called Perah meaning 'wild'.

They live in small groups of five or six in semi-desert which can reach temperatures of 49°C. They feed on grasses, herbs and shrubs and never move too far from a watering hole. The Onager is now an endangered species and in 2005 numbers were estimated at around 600.

Pantelleria

Native to
Sicily

Size
11.3hh - 13.3hh

Description

They are black or dark bay. The short, glossy coat has an oily feel which is unusual in a donkey. The muzzle is a pale grey as are the underbelly and the inner parts of the legs. The tail is bushy.

The Pantelleria donkey dates back to the 1st century BC and is the result of crossing African and Sicilian breeds. I have heard them described as 'slender, elegant and graceful with a gait reminiscent of a camel'. The Pantelleria was important in the growth and development of the island and they were so valued by the peasant farmers that each donkey was given its own stable.

About 20 years ago the last Pantelleria was drowned. A group of nine donkeys were selected and bred in order to remove unwanted genes and recreate the breed. Soon they will be returned to their natural habitat where they will work in a protected area as a draught animal, as tourist transport or be used to fulfil the ever-growing demand for donkeys in Animal Assisted Therapy.

24.

Poitou

Native to
France

Size
13.1hh – 14.3hh

Description

The Poitou is dark brown or black with a naturally long, shaggy coat. They have a white underbelly, nose and spectacle markings with no stripes or cross.

The Poitou (pronounced *pwa-too*) is officially called Le Baudet de Poitou and considered to be one of the rarest donkey breeds. Historians believe this gentle donkey was grazing in France 2,500 years ago. In the Middle Ages to own a Poitou put you among the nobility. The main use of the Poitou was for breeding. They were crossed with the Trait du Poitevin, a French cob, to produce the Poitou mule used in agriculture. At its peak the region was known to produce in excess of 18,000 Poitou mules per year.

Mechanisation meant the Poitou was no longer needed and by 1977 only 44 remained worldwide. Extinction was a possibility. At this point a collection of authorities and enthusiasts came to the rescue of this easy-going donkey. Their latest figures show there are now 400 worldwide of which 180 are pure bred. Their future is definitely looking brighter.

25.

Provence

Native to
France

Size
12.3hh – 13.1hh

The Provence has a dove-grey coat which sometimes has a hint of red or brown. The underbelly, inner forelegs, thighs and muzzle are white. Occasionally they also have a white jaw line and spectacle markings. The forehead, ears and the edge of the eyes usually have a brown-red tint. The legs can have black horizontal stripes. The dorsal stripe and cross are well defined.

The Provence donkey dates back to the 15th century and was named after the region in which it was created. The shepherds of the area developed and improved the Provence until it was ideal for their needs. Their legs are strong and their hooves are slightly larger than usual which makes this docile, sure-footed animal ideal for carrying heavy loads on treacherous mountain paths.

In the late 19th century there were a recorded 13,000 Provence donkeys but by 1993 only 330 existed. I understand that figures have now reached 600 which is an improvement – but there is still a long way to go before the Provence is safe from extinction.

Pyrenees

Native to
The Pyrenees in France
and Spain

Size
11.3hh – 13.1hh

Description

The Pyrenees is mainly black but can also be brown or chestnut. The underbelly is pale grey as are the insides of the forelegs and thighs. This donkey does not have a cross on its back.

Strong, graceful and intelligent – not me, the Pyrenees donkey. For a small farm with poor land, a donkey was the ideal animal to cope with harsh conditions and poor grazing. The Pyrenees was an important partner and worked as a draught animal or in harness, delivering bread or cheese, transporting hay and firewood and bringing ice down from the snowfields.

Until the early years of the 20th century the Pyrenees donkey flourished, but much as with other donkey breeds, numbers declined and in 1990 the numbers reached an all-time low. Today the leisure industry is creating an ideal opportunity for this hard-working animal, transporting tourists to beautiful, but otherwise inaccessible areas. It has the ability to carry a quarter of its own body weight so will carry the camping equipment of four people.

27.

Ragusano

Native to
Sicily

Size
13.1hh – 14.1hh

Description

The Ragusano is dark bay with a pale grey muzzle and spectacles. The underbelly is a lighter brown and the mane and tail are black.

The Ragusano is a newly established breed created by crossing the Pantelleria, the Martina Franca and the Catalan. It was officially recognised in 1953 by the l'Instituto di Incremento Ippico di Catania (Equestrian Development Institute), which keeps the population records and has laid down the breed standard.

In the early days the Ragusano's ancestors would be used in agriculture and for breeding mules which were ideal for winding mountain paths and frequently used by the military. The Ragusano has all the attributes of its ancestors and can live for up to 45 years.

In recent years donkey's milk has been re-discovered as an anallergic (not allergic) food which is almost identical to human milk and has been found to be suitable for children with food allergies. The milk is also used to produce creams, soaps and moisturisers for the beauty industry.

28.

Romagnolo

Native to
Emilia Romagna in the
Forli province of Italy

Size
13.2hh - 14.1hh

They are dark bay with a pale grey underbelly and muzzle. There is white on the inner legs, throat and inside the ears. They have a dorsal stripe and cross and dark stripes are occasionally found on the legs.

The Romagnolo donkey is the native breed of Emilia Romagna in Italy and dates back to the 5th century. It was once widely used as a pack animal, under saddle and in agriculture because they are strong, willing and reliable with a lively character.

One of the major causes of the decline in numbers was the depopulation of the area. The existing workforce in agriculture aged while the younger generations left the areas to find work. Demand for the Romagnolo decreased. The decline continued into the 1970s when it was threatened with extinction. There is now a breeding programme in place and the Romagnolo is put to work maintaining forests in the mountainous areas which are difficult to use for agriculture but are important to keep the ecosystem in balance.

29.

Sardinian

Native to
Sardinia

Size
7.3hh – 10.3hh

The most common colour is grey with a lighter underbelly, inner thighs and muzzle. The edges of the ears are dark, as are the tips of the mane. They have a dorsal stripe, cross and horizontal dark stripes on their legs.

Much of the early history of the gentle Sardinian donkey is known through the writings of the Jesuit Priest Francesco Cetti in 1774 and the breed has changed very little since then. Do not be fooled by its diminutive size. This is a strong and hard-working animal which is ideal for use in steep, narrow passages and hills, yet strong enough to carry agricultural equipment and water to towns and villages.

The Sardinian donkey has been working on the island for over 2,500 years but for the last 20 has been considered critically endangered by worldwide animal welfare lists. Numbers of the pure-bred Sardinian are still falling. In 1965 there were 27,000 registered but in 1995 there were only 150. The increase of cars and general mechanisation are the main reasons for the decline.

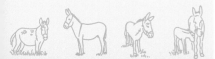

30

Somali Wild Ass

Native to
The southern Red Sea area of Eritrea and the Afar region of Ethiopia and Somalia

Size
12hh – 14.1hh

Description

The Somali Wild Ass has a short, smooth coat which is light grey to fawn, shading to white under the body and on the legs. The mane is thick and upright with black tips, and the ears are large with fluffy black edges. The legs have horizontal black or dark brown stripes like a zebra. The tail has a tuft at the end.

The Somali Wild Ass is a sub-species of the African Wild Ass which in turn is thought to be the wild ancestor of our domestic donkeys. They graze the wild, low scrubland and rocky terrain of eastern North Africa wherever there is access to surface water. They find whatever cover they can during the midday sun, preferring to feed in the early morning and late afternoon. The Somali Wild Ass tends to be a solitary animal primarily due to lack of food. The small herds that do gather tend to be females and young.

Today they are a critically endangered species with less than 300 animals in their native land. In years past, the killing of a Somali Wild Ass was a serious crime and it was decreed that the killer's hand would be cut off.

31

Zamorano Leones

Native to
Northern Spain

Size
13.1hh – 15hh

Description

They range from brown to black. The underbelly, inner thighs, spectacles and muzzle are pale grey. The winter coat is coarse, thick and long while the summer coat is short and smooth. The ears can have long light-coloured hairs hanging from the front.

This powerful donkey is derived from crossing the original local Spanish breeds with those imported from the Catalan region during the 16th century. The breed was originally used for farming and mule breeding and its long winter coat was used to make blankets. It is an animal that adapts well to marginal land where grazing tends to be poor.

The Zamorano Leones suffered from mechanisation in farming and numbers decreased dramatically. In 1982 it was classed as endangered. The Military Stud has a number of these donkeys and it is hoped that, with further research and help from the EU, disaster may be avoided.

The breed has recently started to be used in equine therapy to help children with varying disabilities.

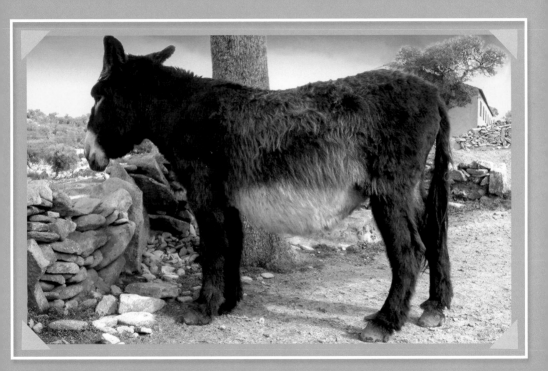

32

Zeedonk/ Zonkey

Native to
Most continents

Size
Varies

Description

The Zeedonk or Zonkey is mainly grey or brown with zebra stripes.

The Zeedonk is a hybrid, the cross between a donkey and a zebra. I am reliably informed that a Zeedonk is the cross between a female zebra and male donkey while the offspring of a male zebra and a female donkey is known as a Zonkey. These hybrids are usually sterile and seldom occur in the wild.

The Zeedonk pictured is a past resident of Colchester Zoo and the result of a cross between a female black ass and a passing zebra.

Other zebra hybrids include a zebrula/zorse – the cross between a female horse and a male zebra, and a zibrinny – the cross between a male horse and a female zebra.

What is a Mule?

According to the popular saying, 'Mules can do anything a horse can do and they usually do it better and with a sense of humour'.

The mule is a cross between a male donkey and a female horse. Mules come in all sizes and can be almost any horse colour except pinto. The offspring of the complementary breeding, between a female donkey and a male horse is called a hinny. All male mules and most female mules are infertile.

Mules are not, as is commonly believed, stubborn or stupid but highly intelligent, rugged and sure-footed. High on a mule's list of priorities is self-preservation which I suppose could be looked upon as stubbornness. A mule is able to work in extreme climates which would be well beyond the capabilities of a horse.

George Washington is said to be responsible for having bred the first mules in America using an Andalusian jack which was a gift from the king of Spain. This jack helped create the 58 mules which George Washington had at work on his farm. They went on to become the most popular working animal in America.

33.

Saddle Mule

Home
USA

Size
14.3hh

Colour
Black with four white socks.

Pictured opposite is Eureka. Her father was a black Catalan cross American Mammoth donkey and her mother was a black-and-white paint horse. Mules of her type would be suitable for riding or driving.

The size and strength of a mule depend on the mare. The self-preservation, inherent in all mules, and the sure-footed gait are inherited from the jack. In Spain and Italy pairs of Catalan-bred mules are frequently used for carriage work and will usually cost more than a pair of horses.

Eureka is the great, great grand-daughter of Secretariat, the famous Kentucky Derby winner.

Belgian Draught Mule

Home
USA

Size
Usually around 15hh

Colour
Chestnut with four white socks and a white rump

Description

Pictured opposite is Suburban. His father was a red-roan American Mammoth donkey and his mother was a Belgian Draught horse.

The Belgian Draught Mule is known for its sure-footedness and easy-going temperament. They can stand heat better than a horse and this is why they are used in the Death Valley in south-west USA. They are also the only animal used to haul people and supplies to the bottom of the Grand Canyon since they can cope with the very steep and narrow trails along sheer cliffs. They are extremely intelligent and affectionate.

Mule Racing

Today there about 70 racing mules in America even though the sport is little known outside California. A mule is a better sprinter than a long-distance runner and over a short distance they can outpace Arabian and Appaloosa horses. Mule races normally take place at the end of horse racing events after the thoroughbreds and quarter horses have run. One of the most popular mule races is Winnemucca Mule Race in Nevada.

The best racing mules are female and the best of the best is Idaho Gem, born on the 4th of May 2003. Unlike horses, mules cannot be put out to stud; they are sterile and so unable to pass on their genes to a future generation. Instead, Idaho Gem is the very first cloned equine.

During the research into cloning Idaho Gem, Professor Gordon Woods of the University of Idaho discovered that his work had great significance in learning the causes of certain male cancers. A company has been set up to carry out further research

Donkey Talk

Ass – Another term for a donkey

Burro – An American term for a small donkey

Jack – A male donkey

Jenny (or Jennet) – A female donkey

Colt – A male donkey under one year old

Filly – A female donkey under one year old

Mule – A male donkey crossed with a female horse

Hinny – A male horse crossed with a female donkey

Dorsal Stripe – A dark line running from the top of the head to the top of the tail

Cross – A second line across a donkey's shoulders which intersects the dorsal stripe to form a cross

Spectacles – A term coined by the author to describe the pale rings often seen around a donkey's eyes

Under-saddle – Riding

Hands High (hh) – Donkeys are measured at the withers – the high point where the neck meets the body. They are measured in 'hands' *(hh)*. One 'hand' is 4 inches.